D0873277

We are the Hunger

We are the Hunger

Poems by

Anita Barrows

Kelsay Books

© 2017 Anita Barrows. All rights reserved. This material may not be reproduced in any form, published, reprinted, recorded, performed, broadcast, rewritten or redistributed without the explicit permission of Anita Barrows. All such actions are strictly prohibited by law.

Cover art: *Torrent,* Alice M. Stern, 2015

ISBN 13- 978-1-945752-33-9

Kelsay Books
Aldrich Press
www.kelsaybooks.com

For my grandchildren, Ciel and Dashiell

Contents

BEFORE THE ENDING

AT THE TURNING OF THE TRAIL

Questo Muro

Quando mi vide star pur fermo e duro
turbato un poco disse: "Or vedi figlio:
tra Beatrice e te e' questo muro."
   —Dante, *Purgatorio* XXVII

You will come at a turning of the trail
to a wall of flame

After the hard climb and the exhausted dreaming

you will come to a place where he
with whom you have walked this far
will stop, will stand

beside you on the treacherous steep path
and stare as you shiver at the moving wall, the flame

that blocks your vision of what
comes after. And that one
who you thought would accompany you always,

who held your face
tenderly a little while in his hands –
who pressed the palms of his hands into drenched grass
and washed from your cheeks the soot, the tear-tracks –

he is telling you now
that all that stands between you
and everything you have known since the beginning

is this: this wall. Between yourself
and the beloved, between yourself and your joy,
the riverbank swaying with wildflowers, the shaft

of sunlight on the rock, the song.
Will you pass through it now, will you let it consume

whatever solidness this is
you call your life, and send
you out, a tremor of heat,

a radiance, a changed
flickering thing?

Summer's End on the Kaweah River

Cornstalks swaying in the last hot wind of August

The river low, in places
only an inch of water

edged by a dusty ridge
of exposed jagged rock. Wind

followed by hot sun followed by clouds
stacking to the north, russet air

pierced by the scent

of hundreds of fallen apples
fermenting in dry grass, all
these slowburning afternoons

that end in the end
of summer, sycamore leaves
saturated with light. What was I

looking for, setting out moments ago
in the whole richness

of the season, to come to this place
where the din of grasshoppers
absorbs the fall

and pooling of water, where a husk
of cicada splits open
in my hand, where everything

is about to dissolve
into everything else?

Night Sky

That blaze
before the meteor

melts into nothing
but its own velocity

On the western slope of the Sierra
my children lay in their sleeping bags

among tall trees, summer
after summer, counting stars that fell

Those were the Augusts of their childhood

Whispering to each other
in the cooling air, wondering

if there was anyone
out there in all that night

like themselves, any
wondering eye   As all around them firelights

went out, voices from inside
lightly billowing tents

softened, ceased

Only that we be known
Only that we be seen

Even as a streak on a darkening field

The way we see the split-off rock
hurtling toward us through space

only by the light
of its perishing

Two

Sometimes two
are summoned together

Bone to bone
Soul to soul

But a dry wind
rattles the space between them

and the sound you hear
after a time

is the agony of one thing
trying

to fit itself
to another

Waiting

(1)

Can you feel it, the double shell of the world
closing a little tighter? Autumn. The fine strands of grass
huddle low against cold, weave themselves into each other.
Whatever I was listening for has been lost in the sound
of everything contracting. Doesn't the mole
persist, groping its way to more
penetrable darkness? All morning I swept dry leaves
from the walk, trimmed back the branches
of plum and apricot. *Dark dark the trees* – Wang Wei
thirteen centuries ago – *where the yellow orioles sang.*
An hour's wind and the pavement I cleared
is covered over, How much more
has to fall away before I have nothing,
before my hands let go of all of it –
pruning shears, broom, the life-line,
the love-line, the creases of light,
the memory of abundance?

(2)

Smiles of meeting turned to parting tears – more Wang Wei.
What do we know of the poet, who, at sixteen, was the emperor's
chosen? He passed from favor and was exiled. At thirty he lost
his wife. Childless, he wandered for years among strangers,
wrote long letters at night to a brother he loved,
made peace with loneliness, built himself a small house
next to a river. Aged, unwell, he petitioned the emperor
for his brother to come to him; and, though at last his request
was granted, the mountains proved impassable in winter.

His brother arrived months later, found Wang Wei's house
abandoned, his path overgrown, apricot petals
falling into a pair of slippers left by the door.

(3)

My friend and I heard two owls calling to each other
through dense eucalyptus, in mist that was almost liquid.
Three notes in a high voice, three
responding in a lower voice. Between: silence,
which, as we listened, grew each time
less bearable. It is all of us
waiting, we said, and never knowing; the brokenness
of the world rushing into the interval
before some answer comes, if it comes. We stumble
a few steps further through brambly underbrush. Chill,
pungent air. Somewhere hidden from us
a small throat opens, staves of a ribcage
expand one more time
with breath. Anguish
holds itself back a little longer.

(4)

Cries of wild geese at dawn. Wang Wei at the window
of his wooden house, a sky the color of wing or ash.
No daylight yet. No sound after the geese call out
their crossing, but the continual drone of the river
widening its passage through rock. Did the air,
too, soften and part? Did a space open up,
where Wang Wei believed
that what would come next, making its way

down the mountain, would be the brother he longed for?
Magnolia bud. Fragrant blossom of acacia. The world
that returns and doesn't return. No footfall
from the snow-covered path. No voice.
No messenger; but grass pressed down by ice
that melts as morning ripens. Slowly
outside the poet's house each straw-colored blade
unbends, stands up, remembers.

Tent

My old blue tent rises on uneven ground,
staked tenuously against a wind
blowing off frozen buttes – held

by some twine I found
and some eight-inch metal hammered down
into dry dirt, among the busying of insects.

I have enclosed a space
which shadows of pinoak and red madrone will reinhabit.

Those I love
are still asleep, near me
and in places I'll go back to. There is a breathing of things

that comforts me. What I'm tethered to
crumbles, but not yet, not now. My living, too,

which I love

is nothing more than an enclosure
around a silence

where the intricate slow labor of breaking down
is all that continues.

Heron

The day my mother died
I saw a blue heron
fly from the branches of a cottonwood,
spread her great wings
over the river, turn east
toward the mountains..
I did not think, *This is my mother's soul*
or *This bird was sent to me*
 as a sign from my mother.
My mother was not a happy woman, not
a woman whose spirit would call to itself
the wildness of birds on a late afternoon
at the end of May in the southern Sierra,
my daughter and granddaughter napping
in the cabin in the sudden heat, the air
rattled with the sound of grasshoppers and cicadas
and I, motherless and alone, walking among dry grasses.

IN TIME OF WAR

Poem in Time of War

1.

She reaches in sleep
for her brother's hand.
Her small fingers grasp his smaller fingers.
She would crawl into the place
where he lies, so untroubled.
His sleeping is deeper than hers.
His dreams are not shattered, like hers,
by planes that fly overhead,
explosions that go on
all night, all day.
He is too young to know
any pain but his own;
and this, if he is safe,
keeps him safe.

2.

We used to sit on the roof
and watch stars
appear, one by one.
Stars
that are made
of nothing but burning.

3.

My father my cousin my aunt
Another cousin my neighbor my brother's friend
A man who used to sell chickens at the market
Another man who drove a taxi:

Every day the list changes, who is alive
and who is dead.
Like a bus: people get off, new people get on
and the bus keeps traveling
through ruined streets, taking its detours.
And I still alive, I am
riding, riding

4.

I did not know what to do with myself
when I could no longer leave my apartment.
Those were the weeks of curfew.
I spent hours setting things in order:
rows of plates, glasses.
I heard them rattle when bombers passed over;
but the bombs that week and the next weeks
were not for me. Mine
was the apartment with books
lined alphabetically on the bookshelves.
Mine were the hands that chopped
garlic, parsley, sweet peppers
gathered from pots
that still stood on the terrace.

5.

We were going to the harbor to watch the boats.
This was something we used to do on weekend afternoons.
That day we couldn't find the street
we had always walked, the narrow street that led,
winding past gardens, down to a place

where everything at last opened blue
and you could see the water.

One street had begun to resemble another.

A dog who once belonged to someone
was eating garbage, and worse.

Between naked rebar
we saw the sails of one boat
stiffening in wind.

6.

The boat is going nowhere
and where it is anchored is also nowhere.
War has made everything the same and nothing.
Come into my dream, it's quiet here.
Do you remember a morning in April?
Do you remember a conversation we had,
leaning over a café table? Music, sweet pastries.
Our heads nearly touching.

7.

Come into my dream:
I am invited to dinner,
though I belong quite possibly
to the legions of the enemy.
The woman of the house
is stuffing zucchini, having cored
each one with a sharp, slender instrument.

She is steaming rice
mixed with cashews, dates.
I sit in another room, talking with her daughters,
listening to the sounds of cooking:
metal lids placed on metal pots,
long spoons rhythmically stirring.
One of the daughters leaves, returns in a moment
with kohl, dark red lipstick.
She takes my face in her hands
as if she could love me.
Let me make you beautiful, she says.

8.

Think now
of this small boy
who has had so many seizures
he can't walk or talk.
All day and all night his brain
is an occupied city, smoldering meanings.
His sisters carry him
as though he were a doll
or a broken kitten.
One of them finds a plastic hairbrush
split in half. She brushes
her brother's hair
with the pink half-brush
and he smiles, smiles.

9.

When the war is over, that's when
the real war will begin.
When everyone else has forgotten

there was a war, when the news is talking
about other wars. When the war is over
there will be the war of remembering
and forgetting, the war
of trying to sleep and trying to awaken, the war

of standing each morning at the window
where sunlight still enters and floods the room

and looking outside
one more day

at all that is not there to return to.

10.

She reaches in sleep
for her brother's hand.
His sleeping is deeper than hers.
He is one of thirty-six children
killed in a single night in a building in Qana.
He is one of fifteen children
killed in a week in Rafah, Gaza City, Balata.
He is one of a thousand children
killed in any season
in the first years of the twenty-first century.
She reaches in her sleep
for the brother who always slept
beside her. She reaches for her brother and he
is not there, he is not even
under the earth.
She reaches in her sleep
for the brother who used to throw
the covers off.

So uncovered.
So uncovered.

11.

Whom, what
do I propitiate here?
The god of chaos?
You who are sometimes called tragedy?
Are you asking me
to offer you my fires, my tamed birds, my firstborn?

12.

Are you listening? Do you know
that the hands that carefully core the soft flesh
of the zucchini
may, at any moment,
even as the zucchini
simmer in their pot of oil,
be struck useless
by a history in which
they have no part?

13.

My granddaughter's friend
to my granddaughter
in the car
on a Wednesday afternoon in California
coming home from ballet class:
"Are there still wars going on?"

And my granddaughter, six, chewing
her raspberry jelly candy,
holding her bright pink baseball cap
in her hands,
"There are always
wars going on."

  —Berkeley, 2006

Flesh and Grass

All flesh is as grass
  —1 Peter 1:24-25

1.

A row of graves in August sunlight.
Some filled, some waiting to be filled.
On the hills, cypress and oleander. A boy
sixteen years old
dug one of these graves a week ago:
chest bare, heavy shovel pushed with his foot
over and over into jagged earth.
When it was finished he leapt inside, joked
with his friends, "This one's
for me." A week later
they carried his body to just
that grave, covered it with the dirt
he had shoveled himself.

2.

How, when his mother
stepped into the street
after hearing the gunshots, the gathering crowd,
the women wouldn't look at her.
That's how she knew it was her boy
who had been killed.

I am listening now
to the Requiem Johannes Brahms wrote
after the death of his mother. *All flesh,* he wrote,
taking the verse from the Bible, *is as grass.*
How there is always a green tenderness

to the body, how delicate it is and how
quickly it passes.
The mother –
not Brahms', the boy's mother –

pushing her way past neighbors, children,
soldiers still standing at the end of the street,
pointing their guns, warm afternoon wind
gathering from the fields beyond the houses.

So much blood
in the dust on the road, searing
heat and the grass behind her
bending, waving.

 —Bethlehem, 2009

Yizkor

Mourner's service
The law enjoining us

not to remain so long in sorrow
that we neglect to dwell also

in gladness

.

Do we beseech?
Whom, what
do we beseech?

Ana, ana – please, please
The Hebrew more like an infant's cry

than a word

.

One bird singing along the western loop
of the Canyon Trail

One bird in the wet early morning

Unseen, hidden among the tangle

of blackberry, manzanita

One bird among liquid flames
at the tips of leaves: singing

Singing   Repeating his song

.

Children watching

as other children
lie dying

in streets where yesterday
they were kicking a ball

A girl watches at the window
while her grandfather goes
to buy bread

An old man
crossing a narrow street

Four in the afternoon

These are the facts
the girl tells the reporters:

How she watched them turn over his body

How they counted the bullet holes: thirty-seven

This and other numbers: her age,

for instance, which is twelve
How many days it had been

since any of them, even the youngest,
had stepped outside

.

…and fields where cattle grazed
strafed with landmines

Still the snow melts in the afternoon sun
Still the new grass comes up

Sparse though it is

.

Outside his tent, in freezing rain,
a man is digging a grave for his son,
who lived four months

What he knew of this world was fear, cold, hunger
His parents' fear   His parents' hunger

His father is on his knees on the hard
ground, softened a little now by rain

There is mud on his clothes and on the cloth
in which he has wrapped the child

He was here for such a little while; he needs
a grave no bigger than his father

can dig with his hands

.

. . . and in the camps, where there was no Torah to read from for
Sabbath services, sometimes someone would hold up a young child
and carry him among the others, who would touch the edges of
their shirts to the child's living body

as they would have done with prayer shawls, kissing them first,
bearing the kisses of their mouths to the Sacred Word

.

In the frost one year when I lived on the hillside
the great eucalyptus died   Long bodies of trees

stood dry, were cut, were carried away
See how many eucalyptus have arisen!

See how the mourner's prayer
must be a prayer of praise

Of renewal

.

Let the words of our mouths
be as flame

rising from ruined lands, flame
rising from flame, undiminished

It is night here, daytime there
where bombs are exploding

What sort of daylight, with everything on fire?
What sort of heat rises from lives that burn?
Let the words

of their mouths pass
into my words

Mouth to mouth

Flame to flame

Cloth

1.

I would make a poem as soft and durable as this cloth

to wind in long sensuous folds,
drawing in and out –
like weaving, like carding wool –

in such a way as to wrap
all of it

into itself

Every end   Every tassel

2.

I would make you a poem
to lay as a cloth on the cold ground
The earth that hesitantly surrenders night to day

Sit on this cloth, set upon it
bread and fruit
Wear it as a shawl upon your shoulders

Set it as a seal upon your forehead
and around your arm

Until the sun is high enough to warm you

3.

as noon approaches,
wear it as a shield

against too much light

Against wind
Against sand
Against dust from roads
traveled by Jeeps, tractors, bulldozers
Cover with this the frayed, the broken places

Cover the scars

4.

Or wear it low on your hips as you dance
to music you turn up loud

in the hour when you need
not to hear anything except that

and the sound your feet make
on the wooden floor

5.

May you shelter yourself
from the eyes of those
who look on you
scornfully

May you hold this cloth aloft
in the dazzling morning

and wave to one you love
across all that is lost and burning

Saying *Here I am*
Even now   Even here

6.

Lay this over the bodies of your dead
Wrap your dead in this cloth as a shroud

Wrap it around the living child

Carry him on your back
His heartbeat bound tight across the vertebrae
that hold you up

7.

Wipe blood from the ground the head the chest the hands

Cover the shame of this woman
walking home

through blind streets

Her skirt torn
Her blouse torn

Wipe the blood from between her legs

8.

Use this cloth as a rug

to cover the floor of this house
that no one can leave or enter

Soldiers
have occupied the rooms

that held the muted cries of lovers
First cries of infants

Mornings and evenings
the songs of thrushes

9.

I would press this cloth, soaked in tears,
to soothe the forehead of one
who has listened too long

to gunshots, to bulldozers, to shouted commands

I would wash this cloth,
dip it over and over
in moving water

Cleanse it
of everything but memory

10.

Cast it as a tent

on the ruined land

Cast this cloth as a tent

Though you cannot believe
you might dwell within –

it is only a little cloth, only a square
woven of colored threads –

Though you walk
in ashes, ashes
on your lips

there will be days when a wind
will saturate the fibers of this cloth
with the fragrance of jasmine, wild mint

Nothing will be restored to you

Yet at moments the ground you stand on
may be cooled

by a shadow
moving lightly over jagged stones

SOME LESSONS FROM DARKNESS

The Golden Retriever Speaks to God

for Tara, 8 March, 1998 – 8 February, 2013

Preserve me so she
can trust that her anxiousness
falls on a listening ear. I know, as one
who has always relied on my ears
more than on my eyes,
that not to be able to see
what you want to believe in
is less difficult than to think
you might cry out
in the wilderness some hour
and nothing
will hear you. Preserve me yet
a little while, old
as I am, blind as I am, sore
in my hips and hindquarters as I
am, so that she can preserve
some sense that her words
are, if not obeyed, then at least
considered. Let her go on,
as I do, believing there is
something that holds out
in the darkness an indulgent hand.

Dust

My friend returns with the news that the dead
are not ashes but chalk and bone. Lime-coated creekbeds,
she tells me, dried out at the end of summer.
She has gone up to Tamalpais
to lay a handful of her sister
six inches into the earth,
smoothed pine needles, bay leaves
over the mound, come down
by shaded footpaths they'd walked
together since childhood. The body doesn't burn
like anything else we know:
spent logs whose husks
you'd dismantle with your finger, curled
flakes of paper. Something impenetrable –
a sliver of jawbone? tibia? – survives
to catch the last glint of sun
setting behind the mountain.
Something is left that the soft, stirred-up dirt
can cling to.

The Well

Long Island, 1957. A boy named Benny
attempted to leap
over a well his father
had been digging in the backyard.
Fell in, was trapped
between walls of earth.

.

This was how
he was: upright, knees
slightly bent, face pressed
against dirt,
tilted to breathe the air
the rescuers sent down to him
through a narrow hose.

.

For more than a day
the machines kept digging.
It was a race between oxygen and Benny.
It was a race between Benny and cold,
fear, the possibility that digging to rescue him
could make the dirt cave all the way.

.

Where he was trapped there was
only a pencil's width of light.

.

Was there one star he could see,
stopped in the firmament
over his little chink in the earth?

.

His house only paces away.
Benny's mother,
his sister. His dog
so frantic she had to be chained
to keep her from clawing
at the hole
where Benny had disappeared.

.

His father out there with so many firemen.

.

By late afternoon the next day
they resurrected Benny,
a shivering, hungry
seven-year old kid
with dirt clogging his mouth,
his nostrils.

.

What helped him,
he said, was that

all that night and through
the urgent morning
he'd been able
to hear

from the surface that was
so near and so
unreachable

their words, the noise
of the machinery
and all
that barking.

Starting with a Bone

1.

Sometimes, on winter afteroons,
my friend Ruthie's mother would make a soup
starting with a bone, a shankbone
the butcher had put aside.
The whole apartment downstairs
would fill with the smell
of onions, celery, potatoes
offering what earth had offered them
to the broth swirling around the heavy bone
that sat at the bottom of the pot.
All those flavors mixing with what the bone,
too, gave forth: bone of this animal
who had lived its life
in a field, a pasture
somewhere we could never imagine, we,
children, waiting to be fed.

2.

I saw a film about a boy

who would have done anything to survive
and did: became traitor, liar, murderer.

Who could judge him? He was a boy.
He wanted to live. He lived.
The fierceness in his eyes

gave way, when the worst was over,
to sadness.

3.

What is hard will be transmuted
to softness, and we say

it is heat that performs
this alchemy, makes space
expand

among molecules, invisible
widen around invisible. What is locked in

begins to emerge. What cannot be eaten

becomes something you could eat.
What is dormant

sprouts green, knows at last
what it has been

created for, gropes its way
into daylight.

4.

....and how sometimes, eating this soup,
you would find in your mouth the bone, a broken-off

piece of it, curiously
tender

How you would crush it between your teeth

and find it not even as resistant
as apples, breadcrust

How it would come apart, then,
on your tongue. How you would taste
the flavor of all it had taken in, flavor
of everything that was

this soup:

vegetable, animal, salt

5.

The film asks whether there is something to choose
that is more than survival.

Is there? Is there something more?

6.

This soup is for those who have not yet learned to grieve

Ruthie's mother, who had been a prisoner in Auschwitz,
never spoke, not even once,
to Ruthie or her sisters

of her first child, their brother, who lay
in a mound of bones

He was an infant under the earth
They were children in Brooklyn, growing tall and strong

7.

The earth is a body of broken bones

8.

He who denies his name
finds his brother again

He who has torn his own flesh
fathers a son

Will you eat this soup?

Who is it
that scatters the ashes, who

will witness the scattering?

What is it
that rises

from all this ruin,
all this ferment?

Lessons from Darkness

Everything you love will perish. Try saying this to yourself
at breakfast, watching the amber-colored tea
swirl in the teapot. Try it on the tree, the clouds, the dog
asleep under the table, the sparrow taking a bath
in the neighbor's gutter. A magician's act: *Presto!*
On a morning you feel open enough to embrace it,
imagine it gone. Then pack the child's lunch:
smooth the thick peanut butter, the jeweled raspberry preserves,
over the bread. Tell yourself the world
must go on forever. Then drive her
to school, imagining the day – orderly –
unfolding. Imagining what you teach her
is true. Is something she will use. This is why,
later, you will go out into the garden
among the calendula, rosemary, hibiscus,
run your finger along the trunk of hawthorn
as though it were the body
of a lover, thinking of the child
on the steps of the schoolyard, eating
her sandwich. Thinking *nothing,*
transparent air, where her hands are.

Light

1.

Her work is the repairing of lamps.
All day she sits on a stool
at the back of the lighting store, connecting wire
to wire, pulling connections apart,
joining them again
in some new way. Testing,
when the last wire is touching the last switch,
to see if the current will run all the way through.

2.

Here is a vocabulary of lamps:
Finial. Switch. Watt.
Socket. Plug.
Shade. Tube. Bulb.
Pole or table.
Harp. Incandescence.

3.

How beautiful your dog's eyes are,
she tells me as she places
my two repaired lamps
in the car. December, nearly six o'clock.
A heavy rain has begun to fall.
She's blind, I tell her. *I can see that,*
the woman says. *Her eyes
are very beautiful.* She has carefully wrapped
the sockets of my lamps
so the rain won't enter. *They are the most*

beautiful part of her, the woman
is saying, *because they are blind. They show
the light of her soul.*

4.

She is Japanese, old enough to have been a child
when the sky lit up on a summer morning
over Hiroshima. She speaks to me
gently, with infinite dignity. She sees the light
in my dog's blind eyes. Spends her days
in silence, with lamps and parts of lamps.

5.

Each of us is a wave, a particle.
My friend, when he went blind at thirty,
learned to see with his hands.
You look tired today, he would tell me,
touching my face.

6.

She must have been three or four.
The war had been going on all her life.
August: a sun exploding
over the earth!
Even if she lived
in another city, she must have heard
the grownups speaking of it.

7.

My dog lies down on the back seat.
Rain streaks the car windows. It's the end
of the day: Lamp
by lamp, she closes her shop.

8.

Where are we going?
Through what kind of landscape?
Into what kind of light?

PSALM

Harvest

In the painting the sheaves of wheat
are leaning into one another.
Yellow sheaves against yellow sky.
You imagine a house. A window
where someone is sitting, watching wheat
move in light wind, making the sound it has always made.

.

You are the painter who has painted this wheat.
Some days you stand in the sunlit room
that is your studio, palette on a paint-stained table beside you.
Yellow is your color, and, after yellow, the blue-violet of twilight.

.

On other days you stand on line at the checkpoint,
papers in hand. It is your name
that is written on them. You are that man
in a gray shirt, dark jeans, a black nylon jacket.
It's cloudy. It's already too late to do
what you were going to do on the other side.
The line is long, the soldier
is letting some go through, turning others away.
It's hard to know whether to stand where you are
or to turn, walk back down the street you came from.
You think of the wheatfield and feel nothing.

.

Why are you attempting to pass
from this place to another?

Whom are you meeting there?
When are you planning to return?
How can we be assured
you are telling us the truth?

The wheatfield darkens. Clouds gather.
Soon it will rain. Soon a man
turned away from the checkpoint
will find a corner of his room, pull a single blanket
over his chest, his face. Will sleep. You too
·will sleep. Only the wheat
will move back and forth in the wind, in the night.

Inspired by the painting *Harvest* (2014) by Fouad Agbaria

Stabat Mater

Vivaldi's *Stabat Mater*
on the CD player, this photograph
in the newspaper on my table:

a refugee woman whose two children have died
stands holding the hands

of two children whose mothers have died

Stabat Mater
And what parched wasted ground

is she standing on, did she
stand on once, and again once, strangled

with grief? She has given these children the names

of the children she lost; their own
names, the newspaper says,

have been forgotten, even by them. They are so
young, they have been walking

for such a long time. *Dolorosa, dolorosa*
the countertenor sings:

the mother stood sorrowing

Psalm

And I would travel with you
to the places of our shame.

The hills stripped of trees, the marsh grasses
oil-slicked, steeped in sewage.

The blackened shoreline, the chemical-poisoned water

I would stand with you in the desolate places, the charred places,
soil where nothing will ever grow, pitted desert;

fields that burn slowly for months, roots of cholla and chaparral
writhing with underground explosions

I would put my hand
there with yours, I would take your hand, I would walk with you

through carefully planted fields, rows of leafy vegetables
drifting with radioactive dust; through the dark
of uranium mines hidden in sacred gold-red mountains;

I would listen with you in drafty hospital corridors
as the miner cried out in the first language

of pain; as he cried out
the forgotten syllables of his childhood

I would be with you
when the radio announced

the dreaded news, I would sit with you

in the chill drizzle, as the heavy trucks
carried before us the heavy

cargo of death; I would stand
next to you in the forest's

final hour, in the wind
of helicopter blades, police sirens

shrieking, the delicate
tremor of light between

leaves for the last
time   Oh I would touch with this love each

wounded place

January Night

Tired of listening to those
who see nothing but darkness
I walk out with my old dog
under the stars
to the grassy place
at the top of our hill
where our days end
and begin. I look out
at the shimmering city
and up at the stars
that are also shimmering.

BEFORE THE ENDING

Two Songs

Black Sow

Marguerite, feed now the black sow
—Ravenscroft Manuscript

Let those who are hungry eat
Let the mist rise from the grass

and the grass be soaked, though there is not yet rain.

Let the grain spill abundantly from the hands
of Marguerite your servant, who only

once the pigs have been fed
may sit down at the table.

The leaves of the quaking aspen are radiant yellow
before the first frost; then
brown, brown as any leaves.

Come, sow. Come, sorrowing one, despised one.
Aren't you lonely out there,
lingering over whatever it is that keeps you?
Though you are not graceful, I see
where your softness reveals itself

between the coarse black hairs

Come for your supper now. Call
every animal in from the fields.

Who does not come will not eat. A wind
darkens the water of the pond.

Here is the day's slop:
hours spent looking out a window,
a letter not written work unfinished.
Someone's hand on a table, absently drumming.

Come from the far place
where you have been poking all morning and afternoon

in cold mud, in stony earth.
Come, black sow. Come, night;
come, sadness. Come, birds

lifting into the sky from the tips of the grasses.
Don't you believe

we have something yet to give you?

Haida Haida

> Haida Haida Haididda Haida
> —Niggun

The song has no words.

It is simpler to speak to God without words.
It is simpler, when the body is tired,
to close your eyes

and let the syllables
ride the crest of melody

faster and faster

surging against whatever it was within you
that kept searching for meanings.

(*in the nursing home*)

One sang in a cantor's choir when he was a boy.
One played piano in nightclubs.

Another gets up from her seat
and thinks she is heading to the subway.
So many nights after work, riding the A train
to the outer boroughs.

Platforms where tired men leaned against white tile walls,
chewing gum, reading the paper, watching

down the long thundering tunnels
for the approaching light.

In the end as in the beginning,
only these syllables?

.

Always I have thought, singing this song,
that the first part is full of tears

as though the one singing it
were singing

after some great loss

.

As though
looking out through a window

onto a known street
which is not the street

that is there, but another,

half-remembered

.

And the second part!
In the second part

you lift your head from where you have cradled it
in your folded arms

You move your head from side to side

and this makes the street dance
through the glass before you

Suddenly you know you are singing
because everything is lost
and lost again

Yet the syllables do not cease their longing
The syllables rise, reach outward, insist

Before the Ending

Later, when we think back
to this time

we will say we did not look long enough

at the mothlike insects swirling at noon
under the branches of the redwood, flaxen wings

catching the sun   We will say
we did not practice one another's languages,

we did not learn to listen
beyond the noises we made, for the small

insistent stirrings
of those who wanted us to know them.

We lived, arguing and imagining.
We thought our lives were separable

from the life of the cornstalk, the many-eyed bluebottle.
How will we explain this? Who

will be there to hear us? We staggered
between our hunger and our confusion.

We traversed the breathing grass
on roads we believed in. Now and then

we were pierced by a startling immensity.

Will anyone ask us, will we ask ourselves

why we did not sit patiently enough

quietly speaking together or in silence,

watching the shifting mosaic
of leafshadow on leaf,

stroking the dog's
broad silken head, gathering

what abundance there is – the grass

bleached in places
but strewn with fallen plums –

tasting the sweetness still with us to be tasted.

Anam Cara

*a Celtic tradition holds that, before differentiated life came to
be, everything was the unified clay of earth*

1.

Once we lay together
in the earth,

part of the earth.

For a long time
we revolved, clay

suffused with clay,
undemarcated, wordless.

My hands

that were not
yet hands

mingled with yours, a surge
of undulant blind roots

slowly veining the dark, thinning
over the dayless nightless ages

to wrist, thumb, forefinger.
Tendril. Stem. Where there was only

a single substance
came a steady pulse of holding and opening,

a rustle of forgetting and wild growth.

So we found
we had been given eyes. We disentangled ourselves

from each other
and stood. We shook off

the body that clung to us.

2.

We came into a century of fire.
We ate. Weren't we hungry? The incinerator-smell

was all around us, the tips of flaming trees
like stars in the amber haze over the city.

We kept looking for home.
We passed one another on rainy streets,

from the windows of trains
flashing by in opposite directions.

We drove ahead of each other through darkened tunnels,
checking the rearview mirror for a hand

raised a little from the steering wheel
in a gesture of greeting, of recognition.

So much we threw into the fire.
At the tables of those

who had nothing else, we broke

contaminated bread. We were hungry,

we ate. We planted plants we were told
leeched poisons from the soil. We did not know

that always, in everything we did,
we were seeking, we were approaching

each other. We listened
for what was still alive. Sometimes

the odor of burning was masked
by a fragrance of orange blossom, acacia.

Sometimes, though the fields
we moved through

were thick with smoke,
it seemed to us we were streaming

through corridors of light.

3.

Earth of whom we are born. In whose body
we ache and burn.

I found the raccoon skull at the edge of the trail,
rim of the eye socket
brittle as dry leaves. It came apart

in my hand. Your hand

reaches for mine: water, carbon,

other minerals. Our bodies are movement and tug
of gravity, fields of grasses and wind

combing the fields. Everything we touch

is a shape held together
by its own stubborn wanting. Oh look at the light

streaming between the branches,
igniting the leaves

of the philodendron. They are turned,
they are made

to receive it in just
that way. And isn't the sunlight,

too, longing to be that
greenness? We are

the one who desires,
the object

of desire, and desire itself.
We are the food and what eats it,

and we are the hunger.

Set Fire

Evidently the only way to find the path
is to set fire to my own life.
—Rabindranath Tagore

Near Temecula, lying under the stars,
I heard coyotes sing; and in the morning
saw the prints of their paws
and the pawprints the dogs made
running after them. The sky
precipitous, millions
of white flames. Yesterday,
in my own house, I wept, thinking
of the singing I have not
followed. So many times
I have turned away, tracks
reversing themselves
in soft dirt. A minute later
I was watching the dogs
wrestle a hose in the garden,
droplets budding on water-darkened
muzzles. Sunlight fell
on Braeburn apples, on ripe
purple grapes in the fruit bowl,
on a blue glass with a little
crescent of milk on its rim
my daughter's lip had left
at breakfast. Must I set fire
to my life, to find my way
to the shimmering
blind core? I love
my life, each thing
in my life, what
is it then I will have to
burn to the ground?

Some Trees

1.

In the long months of listening to reports of war
I grew more and more attached to the Douglas Fir
we planted in the northwest corner of the garden
one winter my children were young. Mornings and evenings
I went out, waiting for something to come to me
from between the branches, watching juncos and towhees
leave and alight. Wanting to be bird or tree,
solid or flickering. Weightless or rooted.

2.

Tell me about the life cycle of trees, how far
under the earth their roots grope,
how broadly beneath the neighborhood
they range: a whole world
below us, probing and grasping, settling and holding fast.

3.

I dreamed someone had split it in half.
Its savaged trunk was red at the core.
Overnight, beetles and ants
had made it their home.

4.

Some trees owe their lives to fire.
Fire opens the seed cone, generative.
Others perish. Still others
persist, grow taller, sprout

new green growth. Live on,
bearing the memory
of inexorable heat, the charred
black wood.

5.

How did you survive? the woman is asked
whose legs were blown off in a bombing.
How did you survive? the child is asked
who fled his burning village.
How did you survive? the soldier asks the brown and white dog
who came to him one day in Kabul and never
afterward left his side. *How? How did you? Did you?*

About the Author

Anita Barrows was born in Brooklyn in 1947 and moved to the San Francisco Bay Area in 1966. She holds Master's degrees in English and Italian Literature and a PhD in Psychology. Her translations of poetry, plays, fiction and non-fiction from the French, German and Italian have been published in this country and in Great Britain; most recently, she has collaborated with Joanna Macy on translations of three volumes of work by Rainer Maria Rilke. Six volumes of her poetry have been published, including a previous book, *Exile,* by The Aldrich Press. Her poems have appeared in numerous journals, including *Tikkun, The Nation, Prairie Schooner, Bark,* and *Bridges*. Barrows lives in Berkeley, where she is a professor at The Wright Institute and maintains a private clinical practice. She is a mother and a grandmother and lives with a menagerie of dogs, cats, and birds.

Made in the USA
Middletown, DE
08 February 2021

33373245R00050